DEADLY CREATURES

DEADLY MAMMALS

ANITA GANERI

PowerKiDS press
New York

Published in 2022 by The Rosen Publishing Group, Inc.
29 East 21st Street, New York, NY 10010

Originally Published in English by Haynes Publishing under the title:
Deadly Creatures Pocket Manual © Haynes Publishing 2019

Cataloging-in-Publication Data
Names: Ganeri, Anita, 1961-.
Title: Deadly mammals / Anita Ganeri.
Description: New York : PowerKids Press, 2022. | Series: Deadly creatures
Identifiers: ISBN 9781725331754 (pbk.) | ISBN 9781725331778 (library bound) | ISBN 9781725331761 (6 pack) | ISBN 9781725331785 (ebook)
Subjects: LCSH: Dangerous animals--Juvenile literature.
Classification: LCC QL100.G35 2022 | DDC 591.6'5--dc23

Design: Richard Parsons

Photo Credits: Cover Shutterstock.com; pp. 5, 23 D&R Halfacre, p. 7 https://commons.wikimedia.org/wiki/File:African_buffalo_Syncerus_caffer.JPG; pp. 9, 10, 13, 15, 17, 21, 29 iStock; p. 11 https://commons.wikimedia.org/wiki/File:Bengal_Tiger_India.jpg; p. 16 https://commons.wikimedia.org/wiki/File:Brown_Bear_Feeding_on_Salmon_1.jpg; p. 19 Claire Waring; p. 24 https://commons.wikimedia.org/wiki/File:2_Panthera_leo.jpg; p. 25???; p. 27 https://commons.wikimedia.org/wiki/File:Ursus_maritimus_4_1996-08-04.jpg; p. 28 https://commons.wikimedia.org/wiki/File:Polar_Bear_ANWR_3.jpg.

Manufactured in the United States of America

CPSIA Compliance Information: Batch #CSPK22. For Further Information contact Rosen Publishing, New York, New York at 1-800-237-9932.

CONTENTS

LOXODONTA AFRICANA

AFRICAN ELEPHANT

The African elephant is the largest and heaviest land animal in the world. Its huge ears, long trunk, and curved tusks add to its impressive appearance. Due to the destruction of their habitat they often wander onto farmland, where they come into conflict with people. This makes them one of the most dangerous animals to humans in Africa.

VITAL STATISTICS

BODY HEIGHT:	8–13 feet (2.4–4 m)
WEIGHT:	up to 13,250 lb (6,000 kg)
EATS:	leaves, grasses, bark
LIFE SPAN:	50–60 years
HABITAT:	grasslands, forests
DISTRIBUTION:	

WARNING

Elephants do not attack other animals for food. But they can be very aggressive when they are protecting calves or when males fight each other. An elephant warns another animal by trumpeting and spreading its ears. If this does not work, it charges at anything in its path. The elephant can terrify any animal it sees as a threat by growling, roaring, and screaming.

DID YOU KNOW?

An elephant's trunk has around 100,000 muscles in it! The elephant uses it to drink, breathe, smell, trumpet, and pick things up.

DEADLY FEATURES

An elephant's huge size makes it a formidable opponent. Its intelligence and speed make it extra deadly. It can trample and crush any other animal that it sees as a threat. It also uses its tusks as weapons in a fight.

SYNCERUS CAFFER CAFFER

AFRICAN CAPE BUFFALO

Herds of African buffalo wander the savanna, grazing on the grass. These huge beasts are closely related to cows but are considered to be one of the most dangerous animals in Africa. To defend themselves and their calves, buffaloes will stand up to fierce predators, including lions.

VITAL STATISTICS

BODY LENGTH:	up to 10 feet (3 m)
WEIGHT:	660–1,980 lb (300–900 kg)
EATS:	grasses
LIFE SPAN:	around 20 years
HABITAT:	grasslands
DISTRIBUTION:	

HORNED HERD

The buffalo is a large animal with a reputation for being bad-tempered. Sticking together in a herd gives the buffaloes safety in numbers and makes them formidable enemies. Both male and female buffaloes have huge, sharp horns, joined together by a hard plate. The male with the thickest horns leads the herd. Males use their horns to fight each other for mates and to decide who is in charge.

DID YOU KNOW?

The buffalo is known as one of the "Big Five" animals on the African savanna. The other four are the lion, leopard, rhinoceros, and elephant.

DEADLY FEATURES

The buffalo's huge size, power, and speed help it to scare away enemies. Although normally quiet and calm, if it has to fight, the herd can charge at high speed, trampling other animals under hooves and goring them with horns.

PANTHERA TIGRIS TIGRIS

BENGAL TIGER

The tiger is the largest and strongest of all the big cats. This magnificent predator hunts at night, using the camouflage of its striped coat to hide among the shadows. Sadly, the tiger is now endangered because people have hunted it for its skin and body parts, and destroyed its habitat.

VITAL STATISTICS

BODY LENGTH:	up to 10 feet (3 m)
WEIGHT:	220–570 lb (100–260 kg)
EATS:	buffalo, deer, antelope, wild pigs
LIFE SPAN:	up to 15 years
HABITAT:	forests, woodland
DISTRIBUTION:	

INCREDIBLE CAT

The Bengal tiger lives in the forests of India, Bangladesh, Nepal, and China. It lives alone except for when a female has cubs. The tiger marks its large territory with scent to keep other tigers away. It has very strong senses of sight, smell, and hearing that help it to find prey. Tigers can jump over 30 feet (9 m), are good at climbing trees, and, unlike other big cats, are excellent swimmers.

TIGER DANGER

Over the last 100 years, tiger numbers have fallen from hundreds of thousands to fewer than 4,000. This is because the tigers' habitat has been destroyed and they have been hunted for their body parts, which are used in traditional Chinese medicine.

DID YOU KNOW?

A tiger's roar is very loud. It can be heard over a mile (1.6 km) away! This warns other tigers away from one tiger's territory. Like a pet cat, a tiger will purr when it is happy.

TERRIFYING HUNTER

The tiger's strength and speed alone make it a fearsome hunter. Its thick neck and powerful front paws make it strong enough to hold down and drag heavy prey. Its orange and black stripes blend in with shadows of the forest, so its victims cannot see it until it is too late. The tiger lies very still until a victim comes near. Then it creeps slowly forward until it is close enough to jump on its prey and grip it in its jaws.

DID YOU KNOW?

Female tigers have two to six cubs in each litter. The cubs stay with their mother, learning to hunt, for up to three years.

DEADLY FEATURES

The tiger's camouflage means it can take its prey by surprise. It has strong, sharp teeth and claws for pulling its victims to the ground. If the animal is small, the tiger breaks its neck in its powerful jaws. It kills a larger animal by biting its throat.

PUMA CONCOLOR

COUGAR

Cougars live in both North and South America and are extremely adaptable, living in a wide variety of habitats. Also known as pumas or mountain lions, these long, slim cats have sandy brown fur. Their hunting territories can cover hundreds of square miles.

VITAL STATISTICS

BODY LENGTH:	up to 5 feet (1.5 m)
WEIGHT:	up to 265 lb (120 kg)
EATS:	deer, moose, birds, mice, porcupines
LIFE SPAN:	up to 13 years
HABITAT:	forests, grasslands
DISTRIBUTION:	

COUGAR PREY

A cougar kills prey as large as moose and caribou, or it will eat small animals such as birds, fish and squirrels. The cougar stalks its prey at night and leaps out when its victim gets close. One bite can be enough to break an animal's neck.

DID YOU KNOW?

When a cougar makes a large kill, it drags the dead animal to a hiding place and covers it with leaves. Over the following days, it returns to its hiding place to eat more of its kill.

DEADLY FEATURES

The cougar's long, strong back legs help it to sprint and jump quickly after prey. Its powerful jaws and long, sharp teeth give its victims little chance of escape once they are in its grip.

URSUS ARCTOS HORRIBILIS

GRIZZLY BEAR

Brown bears live in many parts of the world. The grizzly bear is a brown bear found in North American forests and coastal areas. It has thick fur and a hump of muscle over its shoulders that gives it the power to dig for food. On its hind legs, it stands more than 8 feet (2.5 m) tall.

VITAL STATISTICS

BODY LENGTH:	up to 9 feet (2.8 m)
WEIGHT:	700–1,700 lb (315–770 kg)
EATS:	berries, squirrels, moose, salmon
LIFE SPAN:	20–25 years
HABITAT:	tundra, forests
DISTRIBUTION:	

BEAR HUNT

The grizzly bear has a strong sense of smell that helps it to find food. Their sense of smell is a hundred times better than humans'. These bears spend much of the time eating berries and other vegetation, but they can also eat meat and use their long claws to dig squirrels, marmots, and other animals out of the ground. Other grizzly bears want a bigger meal and hunt for larger prey, such as moose (elk), wild sheep, and goats.

SLEEPING BEARS

In winter, grizzly bears enter their dens and go into a deep sleep. Their body temperature drops and they live off their fat stores. But it is not true hibernation because they can still move around. They wake up the following spring and must immediately start feeding to put on weight.

DID YOU KNOW?

Grizzly bears make dens where they spend the winter. Female bears give birth to their cubs during this time and often have twins.

Grizzly bears get their name from the grizzled, or gray, hairs in their fur.

FISHING BEARS

Many grizzly bears live along the coast of North America. When salmon swim up rivers and streams during the summer, these bears gather along the riverbanks. They use their claws to pull fish out of the water. Sometimes, the bears catch the salmon straight in their jaws as the fish leap up the river. They can eat many fish during this time to build up their fat reserves for the winter.

DID YOU KNOW?

Grizzly bears can run at around 30 miles (48 km) per hour. They are also excellent climbers, so anyone being chased is advised not to try climbing a tree to escape.

DEADLY FEATURES

A female grizzly is at her most deadly when she is defending her cubs. Her huge size and strength are terrifying and one blow from her paws can kill a large animal or human. The bear's long, curved claws are lethal weapons.

PANTHERA ONCA

JAGUAR

The jaguar is the biggest cat in South America. It usually lives in tropical rain forest, where it can climb trees to hide and hunt. Its spotted fur is perfect camouflage as it stalks its prey through the shadows. Jaguars can also have black fur, and these are often wrongly called "black panthers."

VITAL STATISTICS

BODY LENGTH:	up to 6 feet (1.8 m)
WEIGHT:	100–250 lb (45–113 kg)
EATS:	deer, tapir, turtles, snakes, fish
LIFE SPAN:	up to 11 years
HABITAT:	tropical rain forests

DISTRIBUTION:

JAGUAR JAWS

The jaguar has a powerful, muscular body and extremely strong jaws. It lies in wait for prey and jumps out when a victim comes near. The jaguar is a good swimmer and will wait at a river's edge to spring at turtles, fish, and caimans in the water. It can swim carrying a large kill and often drags prey up a tree to eat later.

DID YOU KNOW?

The word jaguar comes from the American Indian word *yaguara*, which means "killer that takes its prey in a single bound." It's a fitting name!

DEADLY FEATURES

The jaguar's stealth makes it a deadly predator. Its teeth are so strong that it can crack open a turtle's shell. It kills many animals by biting right through their skulls.

PANTHERA PARDUS

LEOPARD

ENDANGERED SPECIES

The leopard lives in Africa and some parts of Asia. Its spotted fur makes it very hard to see, as can the fact that it often hides high up in the branches of a tree. It uses its stealth and camouflage to hunt its prey at night.

VITAL STATISTICS

BODY LENGTH:	up to 9.8 feet (2.9 m)
WEIGHT:	80–200 lb (37–90 kg)
EATS:	antelope, wildebeest
LIFE SPAN:	10–15 years
HABITAT:	forests, mountains, grasslands
DISTRIBUTION:	

LONELY LEOPARDS

The leopard usually lives and hunts alone. It is an expert at stalking and hiding from prey, and is well camouflaged. The leopard hunts many different animals, including gazelles, wildebeest, and jackals. It leaps on its prey and bites its throat so that it suffocates. Leopards are very strong and will drag large prey, sometimes three times their own weight, up into a tree to stop other animals from eating it.

DID YOU KNOW?

Some leopards have black fur. They are called black panthers and often live in rain forests and mountains, where their dark fur is good camouflage.

DEADLY FEATURES

The leopard's camouflage makes it very hard to spot. This means that it can creep up on prey without any warning. It also has a massive skull, powerful jaw muscles, and, like all big cats, large, sharp canine teeth.

PANTHERA LEO

LION

The African lion is the only big cat to live in a group, called a pride. In each pride there may be around three male lions and a larger number of lionesses and their cubs. The lionesses in a pride work together to look after their cubs. The lionesses also hunt as a group, and stalk and kill prey for the pride.

VITAL STATISTICS

BODY LENGTH:	5–8 feet (1.6–2.4 m)
WEIGHT:	275 –600 lb (124–272 kg)
EATS:	zebra, antelope, wildebeest, buffalo
LIFE SPAN:	12–18 years
HABITAT:	grasslands, forests
DISTRIBUTION:	

MIGHTY MALES

The male lions in a pride rarely get involved in hunting but they are still deadly. Part of their job is to keep the pride's territory safe from other lions. They do this by marking the area with scent and roaring loudly. Male lions are the only big cats to have manes, which help to make them look bigger and fiercer. They fight each other to decide who is in charge of the pride.

LEARNER LIONS

Lion cubs learn to hunt by play-fighting with each other, pouncing at twigs and trying to catch the end of their mother's tail. They start going out on hunts with their mother when they are about three months old. By the age of two, they can hunt for themselves.

DID YOU KNOW?

When a new male lion joins a pride, he sometimes kills all the cubs. This is to make sure that any new lions in the pride are his own cubs.

TEAMWORK

Lionesses have to hunt together as a team because most of their prey is bigger or can run faster than them. They creep up on a herd of prey animals, such as zebra or wildebeest, crouching silently behind the grass and scrub. Then they slowly move in closer. When they have singled out a victim and surrounded it, one lioness runs in for the kill. Then the others join her to prevent the animal from escaping and to finish the job.

DID YOU KNOW?

Once the pride has made a kill, the male lions get to eat first. The lionesses eat what is left, followed by the cubs.

DEADLY FEATURES

Lions often eat prey that is much bigger than them. To catch and kill large animals, a lion has powerful muscles for running over short distances, strong jaws, sharp teeth, and uses incredible strength to pull down its victim.

URSUS MARITIMUS

POLAR BEAR

The polar bear is the largest bear, and usually lives alone on the ice in the Arctic polar region. It has thick white fur that is water-repellent and acts as camouflage on the ice. Compared to other bears, the polar bear's neck is very long and it has huge, paddle-like feet.

VITAL STATISTICS

BODY LENGTH:	6–8.5 feet (1.8–2.6 m)
WEIGHT:	775–1,200 lb (350–544 kg)
EATS:	seals, walruses, birds
LIFE SPAN:	25–30 years
HABITAT:	Arctic pack ice
DISTRIBUTION:	

SEAL HUNTER

The polar bear's main prey is the ringed seal. These seals swim under the ice looking for fish, but they have to come up to holes in the ice when they need air. The polar bear waits patiently by a breathing hole or a crack in the ice. When it sees a seal come up for air, it pounces. Sometimes, the bear swims under the ice to catch seals or it stalks and attacks them as they rest on the surface of the ice.

DID YOU KNOW?

A polar bear's skin is black under its fur. This helps the bear absorb as much heat as possible in the cold climate. A thick layer of blubber (fat) also helps keep it warm. Its fur is actually clear, but looks white in the light.

UNDER THREAT

Polar bears are in serious danger of becoming extinct. This is because global warming is melting the Arctic ice. The bears depend on the ice for hunting. Without it, they risk starvation unless they can adapt to life on land.

SCAVENGER

Another way in which the polar bear finds food is by scavenging. It often eats the carcasses of dead walruses and whales that have been washed up on the ice, or the remains of other bears' kills. When polar bears find themselves living near humans, they sometimes raid garbage cans to find food. It can be very dangerous for people to come across a hungry bear.

In the Inuit language, the polar bear is called NANOOK. In Inuit mythology, Nanook was the master of the bears.

DID YOU KNOW?

The soles of a polar bear's feet are covered in fur and small bumps called papillae. This helps to keep its feet warm on the ice and stops them from slipping.

DEADLY FEATURES

The polar bear is an amazing hunter. Its powerful sense of smell helps it to find prey, while its white fur provides camouflage as it hunts. It can run and swim incredible distances and has strength, sharp claws, and deadly teeth to destroy its victims.

SARCOPHILUS HARRISII

TASMANIAN DEVIL

The Tasmanian devil is the size of a small dog and lives on the island of Tasmania, off Australia. Stockily built, with dark brown fur, it was given its alarming name because of its extremely loud and terrifying screeching. Despite a ferocious reputation, the Tasmanian devil is actually quite shy and will only aggressively defend itself if threatened.

VITAL STATISTICS

BODY LENGTH:	about 2 feet (60 cm)
WEIGHT:	13–18 lb (5.8–8 kg)
EATS:	dead animals, small mammals, insects
LIFE SPAN:	5–6 years
HABITAT:	coastal heath, forests
DISTRIBUTION:	

DEVIL ATTACK

Tasmanian devils emerge at night to look for food. They hunt small animals, such as possums and wombats, but are also scavengers, locating dead animals with their superb sense of smell. When threatened, a Tasmanian devil "yawns," showing off its powerful teeth. Then it growls, screeches, and attacks.

DID YOU KNOW?

Tasmanian devils are marsupials, like kangaroos, koalas, and possums. Mothers carry their young in a pouch until they are big enough to fend for themselves.

DEADLY FEATURES

Tasmanian devils have powerful jaws filled with sharp, strong teeth for biting through flesh and crushing bones. Their defensive aggression and fierce appearance helps scare away other animals.

GLOSSARY

camouflage to blend into surroundings
endangered in danger of dying out
extinct no longer existing
habitat the place where an animal usually lives
jaws the part of the head in which the teeth grow
reputation the common opinion about something
savanna a large area of grass that's flat and has few trees
scavenge to search for food, usually dead animals
stealth having to do with a quiet way of moving
territory an area in which an animal lives

INDEX